THE LIVING GOSPEL

*Daily Devotions for Lent 2019*

Charles Paolino

Ave Maria Press  AVE  Notre Dame, Indiana

Founded in 1865, Ave Maria Press is a ministry of the United States Province of Holy Cross.

www.avemariapress.com

Paperback: ISBN-13 978-1-59471-849-6

E-book: ISBN-13 978-1-59471-850-2

Cover image "At the Foot of the Cross" © Jeni Butler, artworkbyjeni.wix.com.

Cover and text design by John R. Carson.

Printed and bound in the United States of America.

# INTRODUCTION

In the musical *Man of La Mancha* by Dale Wasserman, the errant knight who calls himself Don Quixote irritates his family with his self-assigned campaign to correct a world he calls "base and debauched as can be." He focuses particular attention on the libertine Aldonza, calling her "Dulcinea" and visualizing her as the ideal of womanhood—a notion she ridicules and rejects.

In an attempt to bring Don Quixote to his senses, a relative of his dresses up as the "Knight of the Mirrors" and confronts the old man, forcing Don Quixote to see himself as the world sees him—namely, as a madman. Don Quixote collapses under this attack, but when he hears the voice of Aldonza, who has realized his decency and her own worth, he rises from his bed and recommits himself to his quest for a better world. Though he dies shortly thereafter, Don Quixote has changed Aldonza's life and left a legacy of integrity and optimism that challenges the cynicism and ambivalence of society.

Lent is like a mirror. The season invites us to see ourselves as we are. The object, however, is not to humiliate us or discourage us; the object is not to deny our intrinsic value. On the contrary, Lent does not concern what we see on the surface when we look in the mirror but rather what we can see if we look more closely.

Lent invites us to see who we are but also, and more importantly, to see who we can be—that is, what we are called to be by God, who dignified human nature by assuming it himself in the person of Jesus Christ. If he was a human being like us, to paraphrase an old saying, let us be human beings like him.

This book of daily reflections and prayer provides an opportunity for you to look in the mirror each day and see what potential is there.

For each day of Lent, there are prompts for prayer, including a passage from the Responsorial Psalm or Old Testament reading of that day's Mass, a few verses from the gospel reading for the day, a personal reflection that draws on the lesson of that gospel passage, a suggested step toward spiritual growth, and a closing prayer. There are also gospel passages, short reflections, and prayers for the Easter Triduum—Holy Thursday, Good Friday, and Holy Saturday.

You may benefit most from this book if you devote about ten minutes to each day's devotion. Committing to the same time of day and the same quiet place can help you establish a rhythm for this part of your Lenten observance. You may spend the time as you wish. You might, for example, choose to read the entire gospel reading instead of only the briefer passages printed for each day in this little book.

What is important is that in spending time with this book you move closer to God, and to the person you want to be, one day at a time, with Jesus as your companion.

# Wednesday, March 6
## Ash Wednesday

BEGIN

*Spend a minute or two in silence. Set aside whatever might hinder your prayer.*

PRAY

Even now, says the LORD, return to me with your whole heart.

*~Joel 2:12*

LISTEN

*Read Matthew 6:1–6, 16–18.*

"When you pray, go to your inner room, close the door, and pray to your Father in secret."

*~Matthew 6:6*

*Your Light Shall Break Forth*

One of the most memorable characters from British television comedy is Hyacinth Bucket, the central figure in the series *Keeping Up Appearances*. The theme of the BBC series, which has also been broadcast in the United States, is that Hyacinth can't accept her social status. She is a woman of average circumstances, but she wants to be a member of the upper crust. So she pronounces her surname "Bouquet" and pretends to be elegant—unaware that she is abhorred by her neighbors and is making a fool of herself.

Hyacinth Bucket is a comic figure, but there is tragedy in her story—and that tragedy is that instead of making her genuine self a gift to those around her, she tries to make an artificially grand appearance and consequently has nothing of value to offer.

In today's gospel reading—from Matthew's telling of the Sermon on the Mount—Jesus cautions us against making a similar tragic mistake in our religious and moral lives. He encourages us to pray, to fast, and to help those who are poor because these things are good in themselves, not because we want others to admire our piety and charity or because we want to become prominent in our parishes or our communities—in fact, not because we expect any reward at all.

When we pray and fast and help those who are in need, we imitate Jesus himself, and we know that Jesus did not do these things in order to attract public approval. In fact, he attracted criticism, rejection, and persecution.

Let us, then, imitate Jesus quietly, modestly, without flourish, without letting the right hand know what the left hand is doing, and leave the rest to God. As today's gospel reading tells us, our Father who sees what is hidden will repay us.

## ACT

*Take a step toward spiritual growth.*

I will set a tone for my observance of Lent by intentionally spending time alone with God today.

## PRAY

Father in heaven, though you are the Creator of the universe, you care for us as your sons and daughters, welcoming each of us into your presence. May the time I spend with you help me to grow in gratitude for your grace and in eagerness to reflect your love wherever I go. Amen.

# Thursday, March 7
## Thursday after Ash Wednesday

BEGIN

*Spend a minute or two in silence. Set aside whatever might hinder your prayer.*

PRAY

Choose life, then, that you and your descendants may live, by loving the LORD, your God, heeding his voice, and holding fast to him.

*~Deuteronomy 30:19b–20a*

LISTEN

*Read Luke 9:22–25.*

"If anyone wishes to come after me, he must deny himself and take up his cross daily and follow me."

*~Luke 9:23*

## *Take Up the Cross*

Marguerite d'Youville, born Marie-Marguerite Dufrost de Lajemmerais in Quebec in 1701, was still a child when her father died, leaving the family in poverty. After briefly attending school, Marguerite instructed her siblings. She was about to marry a prominent young man when her mother wed an Irish-born doctor, disgracing the family in the intolerant community, ending Marguerite's engagement. In 1722, Marguerite instead married a man who illegally traded liquor to native people. He died in 1730, and four of the couple's six children died in infancy.

Despite her misfortunes, Marguerite grew in her faith that God was present in her life and in her determination to be an instrument through which God's love could touch other people. In 1737 she and three other women formed an association that would eventually become the Sisters of Charity of Montreal.

The women opened a home for the poor, an enterprise that was ridiculed by their families and friends. They persisted, however, expanding the capacity of the house. The small community was established as a religious order in 1744 and, in 1747, took over a derelict city hospital, putting it on a sound footing. The hospital burned down in 1765, but under Marguerite's leadership, it was rebuilt. She died there in 1771. A model for us all, Marguerite was canonized by Pope John Paul II in 1990.

Today's gospel reading is clear: disciples of Jesus must imitate him by patiently enduring rejection and ill fortune and bringing God's love to those who need it most, whether the need is material or spiritual. May we, like Marguerite, always strive to do just this.

## ACT

*Take a step toward spiritual growth.*

I will identify a person I know or have heard of who is experiencing need or distress and spend some quiet time imagining myself in that person's position. I will conclude by asking God, if it is his will, to shorten or relieve that person's suffering.

## PRAY

Almighty God, help me to see every person as equally the object of your love and, therefore, equally deserving of my prayers and support. Even as I live in the knowledge of your love for me, may I never forget the limitless love you have for all your children. Amen.

# Friday, March 8
## Friday after Ash Wednesday

BEGIN

*Spend a minute or two in silence. Set aside whatever might hinder your prayer.*

PRAY

Then your light shall break forth like the dawn, and your wound shall quickly be healed.

*~Isaiah 58:8*

LISTEN

*Read Matthew 9:14–15.*

"Can the wedding guests mourn as long as the bridegroom is with them? The days will come when the bridegroom is taken away from them, and then they will fast."

*~Matthew 9:15*

## *The Groom Will Return*

My wife, Pat, and I got married on August 22, 1964. The Mass started at 4 p.m. when the temperature was 93 degrees. It was still nearly 92 degrees when the reception began in a hall that was not air-conditioned.

At first, everyone was uncomfortable. But as jackets and ties were tossed aside, the food and drink appeared, and the music and dancing got under way, the guests seemed to forget about the heat—so much so that Pat's dad paid the band to stay overtime, and the party went on till about 1 a.m.

The exuberance associated with the wedding itself and the gathering of family members and old friends caused the revelers to forget their cares—and even to forget that their cares would be waiting for them tomorrow. Perhaps this is an apt metaphor for the exuberance of the disciples of Jesus who made the most of the time they had with him.

Those who asked why the disciples didn't observe fasts—which, by the way, were traditional but not compulsory in Judaism—did not share in the conviction that he was the unique and irreplaceable manifestation of God. And so they could not anticipate what Jesus was predicting—that he would not always be physically present and that his followers would one day await his return with a combination of anticipation and yearning.

We are among those followers, trying to live according to his teaching and example, because we have faith in his Resurrection and Ascension and his promise to return. Our fasting, during Lent and throughout the year, takes many forms—prayer, self-denial, and generosity with others—as we strive to keep Christ as the focal point and model for our lives so that we will be ready to rejoice when we are at last perfected in his presence.

## ACT

*Take a step toward spiritual growth.*

I will select a small symbol of Jesus—a medal, a crucifix, a prayer card—to carry with me each day; when I see this symbol or feel it in my pocket, I will remember that Jesus is present with me in everything I say and do.

## PRAY

Lord, Jesus, may the gratitude I have for your sacrifice and the faith I have in your Resurrection keep me always focused on you so that all of my decisions and actions reflect your grace to everyone I encounter. Amen.

# Saturday, March 9
## Saturday after Ash Wednesday

BEGIN

*Spend a minute or two in silence. Set aside anything that might hinder your prayer.*

PRAY

Teach me your way, O Lord, that I may walk in your truth.

*~Psalm 86:11*

LISTEN

*Read Luke 5:27–32.*

Jesus said to them in reply, "Those who are healthy do not need a physician, but the sick do. I have not come to call the righteous to repentance but sinners."

*~Luke 5:31–32*

## *Learning from the Poor*

When Greg Boyle was ordained a Jesuit priest in 1984, he was bound for a university campus ministry, but a shortcut through Bolivia changed everything. Fr. Boyle had gone to Bolivia to study Spanish, but—he told Terry Gross of the radio series *Fresh Air*—"it just turned me inside out. I was . . . being evangelized by the poor. I just said, I want to cast my lot with the poorest folks I can find."

When he returned to the States, Fr. Boyle asked his provincial to send him to the poorest place possible; that turned out to be the Dolores Mission in gang-infested East Los Angeles.

In his three decades as pastor there, Fr. Boyle has presided over the burial of hundreds of young people killed by gang violence, but he has also founded a group of businesses known as Homeboy Industries—a restaurant, a bakery, a café, a tattoo-removal service, and farmers' markets. By employing and training former gang members and ex-prisoners, he has helped many hundreds of them make the transition to stable lives.

Fr. Boyle's experience illustrates a lesson in today's gospel reading—prompted by the question, "Why do you eat and drink with tax collectors and sinners?" The lesson is that we cannot evangelize others unless we are present to them.

Perhaps heroism like Fr. Boyle's is beyond our capacity, but we all are called to be missionary disciples of Jesus by leaving our comfort zones and touching the lives of people who are still seeking union with God. We can undertake that mission among the people we encounter in everyday life but who are outside of our parish circle by gently witnessing to our faith with no hint of judgment, inviting others to share what brings us joy, and imitating Jesus, as Fr. Boyle does, with actions of charity, justice, and peace.

ACT

*Take a step toward spiritual growth.*

I will carefully consider where, in my daily routine, there are opportunities for me to directly or indirectly, through word or deed, express to those who are separated from the Church the joy of the Gospel.

PRAY

Lord Jesus, I know that when you called Levi, the tax collector, to follow you, you were also calling me. May I have the courage and prudence to imitate Levi by setting aside anything that might keep me from being your missionary disciple. Amen.

# Sunday, March 10
## First Week of Lent

BEGIN

*Spend a minute or two in silence. Set aside whatever might hinder your prayer.*

PRAY

For to his angels he has given command about you, that they guard you in all your ways.

*~Psalm 91:11*

LISTEN

*Read Luke 4:1–13.*

"It is written: 'You shall worship the Lord, your God, and him alone shall you serve.'"

*~Luke 4:8*

## Be Alert to Satan

On December 14, 1992, Wayne Lo, an eighteen-year-old student at Bard College in Great Barrington, Massachusetts, went about the campus shooting people at random. He killed two people and wounded four others and was ultimately sentenced to two life terms without parole.

Lo said at the time that God had told him to carry out the shootings, but he has come to understand that it wasn't so. Of course, the God who creates all that is, the God who delivered Israel from slavery in Egypt, the God who stepped into human history in the person of Jesus of Nazareth, would do no such thing.

But in today's gospel passage we read about another player, who does do such things. Pope Francis has written about this player: "Evil is not something intangible that spreads like the fog of Milan. It is a person—Satan.

We must discern the lies of Satan—with whom I am convinced there is no dialoguing."

Lo's experience was unusual, but it reminds us that God does not contradict his own law as it is embodied in the Ten Commandments and the Beatitudes. Just as God did not prompt Lo to shoot innocent people, God does not prompt anyone to traffic in drugs; discriminate against others based on gender, race, or religion; put others at risk by driving recklessly; treat employees or customers unfairly; damage or fail to protect the environment; or neglect those who are poor, lonely, or infirm.

If one falls for the devil's hints, one can rationalize such behavior or simply avoid facing the moral issues it raises. The best way to neutralize Satan's influence is to be in dialogue with God—to be aware that he accompanies us, to be at prayer—all day, every day.

ACT

*Take a step toward spiritual growth.*

Today I will spend some quiet time thinking about aspects of my life in which I may be inspired by something other than God—something at odds with God's law. I will ask the Holy Spirit to help me remain alert for such promptings and to resist and reject them.

PRAY

Come, Holy Spirit, fill my heart, and enflame it with faithfulness to God alone. Help me always to turn away from even the most subtle distractions from what is right and just. Amen.

# Monday, March 11
## First Week of Lent

### BEGIN

*Spend a minute or two in silence. Set aside whatever might hinder your prayer.*

### PRAY

The ordinances of the LORD are true, all of them just.

*~Psalm 19:10b*

### LISTEN

*Read Matthew 25:31–46.*

"And the king will say to them in reply, 'Amen, I say to you, whatever you did for one of these least brothers of mine, you did for me.'"

*~Matthew 25:40*

## Did We See You Hungry?

Rummaging in a filing cabinet in a room behind my family's grocery store, I came across some bills that were yellowed with age and dated from the 1930s. These bills indicated that our store had provided meat and groceries to customers, and the fact that the bills were still in the filing cabinet meant that they had not been paid.

I took a few of these bills out of the cabinet and showed them to my father. He told me that during the Great Depression our family still had an income from those customers who still had jobs.

As for those who did not have jobs, Dad said, "They still had to eat."

What has impressed me about that statement is the matter-of-fact way in which my father made it, almost as though it should have been obvious to me.

Of course we fed them. They were hungry.

That seems to have been the attitude of the "sheep"—the righteous ones—in the dramatic picture of the Last Judgment drawn by Jesus in today's gospel passage.

Jesus portrays these generous men and women as being surprised that the Son of Man praises their acts of charity and connects it to himself. The most salient detail in that picture may be the fact that those who are blessed for having fed the hungry and clothed the naked had not done it to impress God and save their souls; they had done it because they wanted to, because it seemed right.

That's a mindset worth cultivating during Lent, the idea that the needs of even our "least" brothers and sisters are as important to us as our own needs. Adopting that mindset means imitating Jesus himself, the One with whom we hope to share eternal life.

## ACT

*Take a step toward spiritual growth.*

I will spend five minutes remembering the joy of doing kindnesses, large and small, for strangers and friends, and I will thank God for acts of kindness, large and small, that others have done for me.

## PRAY

Lord Jesus Christ, you gave us the perfect example of an unselfish life. Help me to imitate you by extending compassion and generosity to those who are close to me and even to those whom I will never meet. Amen.

# TUESDAY, MARCH 12
## FIRST WEEK OF LENT

BEGIN

*Spend a minute or two in silence. Set aside whatever might hinder your prayer.*

PRAY

I sought the LORD, and he answered me and delivered me from all my fears.

*~Psalm 34:5*

LISTEN

*Read Matthew 6:7–15.*

Jesus said to his disciples: "In praying, do not babble like the pagans. . . . Your Father knows what you need before you ask him."

*~Matthew 6:7a, 8b*

## We Ask Nothing More

When the nineteenth-century scientist Charles Darwin was a young man, he collected examples of more than 300,000 species of beetles.

Once, while he was out walking, he spied a beetle of a type he had not yet captured. Unequipped for this, he held the beetle in a closed hand and went on his way. Before reaching home, he spied a beetle of another type and carried that one in his other closed hand. Then he spied a third and, unwilling to waste the opportunity, put that one in his mouth where the understandably annoyed insect excreted a bitter substance that made Darwin spit out the beetle and involuntarily release the ones in his hands.

Whatever lesson Darwin learned from this experience, the rest of us can conclude that trying to hold on to too much at once can leave us empty-handed. That's also the tone of the advice Jesus gave his disciples in the discourse described in today's gospel reading. Jesus' recommendations about prayer, and the Lord's Prayer itself, speak of simplicity—not only simplicity in language but also simplicity in desire.

In this chapter of Matthew's gospel, Jesus, as he often did, recommended detachment; he recommended that we avoid becoming obsessed with material things and the hunger in our souls. The clause "Give us this day our daily bread" is another way of saying, "Give us what we need to live fruitfully and honorably today—we ask nothing more."

This is the poverty of spirit that fasting is designed to inspire in us and that Lent can inspire, whether or not we literally fast. It is, after all, a form of fasting to shift our attention from how we can acquire more than we need to how we can help those who have less than they need.

## ACT

*Take a step toward spiritual growth.*

I will identify one thing that I am likely to buy but don't really need, even if it's not a luxury, and donate the price to a charity.

## PRAY

Our Father, who are in heaven, hallowed be your name. Your kingdom come. Your will be done on earth, as it is in heaven. Give us this day our daily bread, and forgive us our trespasses as we forgive those who trespass against us. And lead us not into temptation, but deliver us from evil. Amen.

# Wednesday, March 13
## First Week of Lent

### BEGIN

*Spend a minute or two in silence. Set aside whatever might hinder your prayer.*

### PRAY

My sacrifice, O God, is a contrite spirit; a heart contrite and humbled, O God, you will not spurn.

*~Psalm 51:19*

### LISTEN

*Read Luke 11:29–32.*

"At the judgment the men of Nineveh will arise with this generation and condemn it, because at the preaching of Jonah they repented, and there is something greater than Jonah here."

*~Luke 11:32*

## Greater than Jonah

The first reading in today's Mass is an account of Jonah's mission to the people of Nineveh. In the interest of time, I suppose, the editors of the *Lectionary* left out the part about Jonah initially running the other way when God told him to go preach to those sinners. And the editors also left out Jonah's reaction when the fish spit him up on the shore, and he did go to Nineveh, and everyone from the king on down actually listened to him and repented.

The passage we read today reports that God was satisfied with their repentance and withdrew his threat to destroy the city. But if we were to read on, we would find that Jonah, far from being satisfied, was annoyed.

He was looking forward to seeing God wipe out the Ninevites, he was frustrated by God's compassion, and he was still sulking about it at the end of the story.

In the gospel reading, Jesus calls his audience to task because the corrupt and depraved Ninevites were converted by the most imperfect of prophets, but the generation of Jesus' time is resisting the most sublime prophet of all: "There is something greater than Jonah here."

Presumably, none of us have sunk to the level of "wickedness" that the scripture attributes to the Ninevites, but it's a rare person who doesn't need to be converted again and again to full, self-emptying discipleship.

Much like the people Jesus was addressing in Luke's account, we hear what Jesus teaches. We hear it in scripture and in the Church's teachings and we encounter him in the sacraments. There may be an occasional Jonah in that ambo, but the Gospel of unqualified love of God and universal love of neighbor comes from Jesus, who is not only greater than Jonah but also greater than anyone or anything else that tries to influence us.

ACT

*Take a step toward spiritual growth.*

I will set aside time to read the Beatitudes (Matthew 5:3–12) and contemplate how they are reflected in my life. Do I strive to live the Beatitudes? Or do I, like Jonah, cling to petty resentments?

PRAY

Lord Jesus, our Teacher, send the Holy Spirit to open our minds to clearly hear your words, and open our hearts to bring your words to life in our acts of compassion and justice. Amen.

# THURSDAY, MARCH 14
## FIRST WEEK OF LENT

BEGIN

*Spend a minute or two in silence. Set aside whatever might hinder your prayer.*

PRAY

When I called, you answered me; you built up strength within me.

*~Psalm 138:3*

LISTEN

*Read Matthew 7:7–12.*

"Ask and it will be given to you; seek and you will find; knock and the door will be opened to you."

*~Matthew 7:7*

## He Hears Us

Perhaps it was because Bill Moyers had been a minister that President Lyndon Johnson once asked him to say grace at a White House dinner. According to the story, Moyers, an assistant to Johnson, complied in a low voice. Johnson bellowed, "Speak up, Bill! I can't hear you." To which Moyers replied, "I'm sorry, sir. I wasn't addressing you."

Of course he wasn't; Moyers was expressing gratitude to God, the source not only of the food on the White House table but of everything that exists.

Gratitude for our lives and for the things we use to sustain ourselves is a primary theme of our prayer. It's the name by which we call the sacrament in which we receive from God the Body and Blood of his Son—"Eucharist," which means thanksgiving.

We also pray to honor and praise God ("hallowed be thy name") and to petition God, which Jesus discusses in the remarks in today's gospel passage. But petitioning God is not like rubbing an oil lamp and asking the genie for three guaranteed gifts. No, in this passage, Jesus emphasizes the need for persistent prayer, not because all our wishes will be fulfilled but because we have faith that God accompanies each of us, all the time.

That's what we read elsewhere in the scriptures, that ultimately we submit our petitions to God's judgment. "And this is the boldness we have in him, that if we ask anything according to his will, he hears us" (1 John 5:14). By telling us three times to pray—to ask, to seek, to knock—Jesus tells us not to turn to God now and then to fill a specific need or desire but to be in constant dialogue with the Father who knows what we need before we ask him (Matthew 6:8).

## ACT

*Take a step toward spiritual growth.*

Each night, I will recall the times that day that I spoke to God or was aware that he was accompanying me.

## PRAY

O God, our Father, thank you for your generous gifts, including life itself, and thank you for being the constant companion of each one of us, not only willing but eager to hear us when we call on your goodness and your mercy. Amen.

# Friday, March 15
## First Week of Lent

BEGIN

*Spend a minute or two in silence. Set aside whatever might hinder your prayer.*

PRAY

For with the LORD is kindness and with him is plenteous redemption.

*~Psalm 130:7b*

LISTEN

*Read Matthew 5:20–26.*

"Leave your gift there at the altar, go first and be reconciled with your brother."

*~Matthew 5:24b*

## Be Rid of Anger

I have been researching my family's genealogy, and I've traced one Italian branch to the eighteenth century. But there is one dead end that was caused by a disagreement among my forebears in my grandparents' generation: members of the family stopped speaking to each other because one of them had Anglicized his surname, and the hard feelings persisted for decades until all of them had died. As a result, one wing of the family was permanently lost to me.

I knew about this disagreement while I was growing up, but I would never have associated it with one of the commandments we memorized in our faith formation: "Thou shalt not kill." It was only when I was an adult and had studied the Catholic faith in more depth that I appreciated the implications of what we read in today's gospel passage: "Everyone who grows angry with his brother shall be liable to judgment."

"You have heard the commandment 'You shall not commit murder,'" Jesus says. We have heard it, and we might think of it as both self-evident and remote from our personal experience. But when Jesus says, in such strong terms, that we also must not harbor anger or hold grudges against each other or even speak harshly to each other—in other words, that this behavior is one form of killing—he is saying something radical.

These remarks from Jesus remind us that being his disciple involves hard decisions about how we live—that we can't fully enter into discipleship while rationalizing any behavior that falls short of unconditional love of others. It is unlikely that we will be asked to look at our persecutors from a cross and forgive them, but we are asked to rise above anger and stubbornness when our relations with others are broken.

## ACT

*Take a step toward spiritual growth.*

If I have a relationship that needs to be mended, I will consider what first step I can take toward reconciliation.

## PRAY

Lord Jesus Christ, throughout your ministry and even on the cross, you set an example of forgiveness and unconditional love. Help me to imitate you in even the trivial disagreements that arise in daily life. Amen.

# Saturday, March 16
## First Week of Lent

BEGIN

*Spend a minute or two in silence. Set aside whatever might hinder your prayer.*

PRAY

Blessed are they whose way is blameless, who walk in the law of the LORD.

~*Psalm 119:1*

LISTEN

*Read Matthew 5:43–48.*

"But I say to you, love your enemies, and pray for those who persecute you."

~*Matthew 5:44a*

## *Too Much to Ask?*

A disgraceful aspect of World War II in Europe was the fact that so many people looked the other way while the Nazis tried to exterminate the Jewish population. However, the French prelate Pierre-Marie Théas was not among them. While he was bishop of Montauban in southern France in the early 1940s, he joined other French bishops in condemning the deportation of Jews to death camps. A pastoral letter he wrote on the subject was delivered by bicycle to be read in forty parishes in France, and it was smuggled to London and broadcast by a BBC service to tens of thousands of listeners in France.

After he delivered a sermon in 1944 condemning the treatment of Jews, he was arrested and sent to a concentration camp at Compiègne, about fifty miles north of Paris, where he remained until the camp was liberated. He urged the other prisoners—who had a hard time accepting it—to pray for their captors, and when he celebrated Mass at the camp, Bishop Théas prayed for Germany.

The fact that such an implacable opponent of the Nazis would ask their victims to pray for them is an apt demonstration of the profound nature of the teaching we read in today's gospel passage. Jesus didn't mean that we should accept bad behavior, but he did mean that we should let go of anger and vengefulness and ask God to touch the hearts of our enemies and lead them to lives of justice. Praying for the well-being of our foes may seem illogical, but it is the logic of the Cross, where Jesus prayed for the Roman soldiers who were in the act of killing him.

Is it too much to ask? Jesus answers that in today's reading: "Be perfect as your heavenly Father is perfect."

ACT

*Take a step toward spiritual growth.*

I will ask God to help me cast off any lingering animosity toward anyone who has harmed me or someone close to me, and I will intentionally offer the next Mass I attend for the offending person's well-being.

PRAY

Lord Jesus Christ, you taught us to love our enemies and pray for our persecutors. May I live by your teaching and follow your example by replacing any animosity in my heart with compassion for those who have offended me. Amen.

# SUNDAY, MARCH 17
## SECOND WEEK OF LENT

BEGIN

*Spend a minute or two in silence. Set aside whatever might hinder your prayer.*

PRAY

I believe that I shall see the bounty of the LORD in the land of the living.

*~Psalm 27:13*

LISTEN

*Read Luke 9:28b–36.*

Peter said to Jesus, "Master, it is good that we are here."

*~Luke 9:33*

## *An Unshod Hillbilly*

During World War II, US Army captain Charles L. Badley wrote home to California about how he and his colleagues had celebrated Christmas 1942. The highlight was that he had been chosen with four other American and British servicemen to have dinner on Christmas Day with Queen Mary—widow of King George V, mother of Edward VIII and George VI.

In sumptuous surroundings, Badley received a personalized gift from Queen Mary plus a memento to send home to his mother, and he dined next to the queen, monopolizing her conversation. The soldier mentioned feeling like "an unshod hillbilly in town for the very first time." The contrast between that gathering and army life could not have been lost on him.

Badley couldn't be blamed if he had wished that the dinner would never end, but he would go back to army cots and army grub and an uncertain future. His feelings might have mimicked those of Peter in today's gospel passage.

Peter knew the hardscrabble life of a fisherman and the hand-to-mouth, risky existence of a follower of Jesus, who was challenging the status quo and rankling the establishment. When Peter, James, and John glanced momentarily at the glory of their Teacher, they were out of their element. All three might have wished that they would not have to climb down from that height and face the challenges of discipleship, but only the impetuous Peter said it out loud.

But everyday life is what discipleship was about for them, as it is for us. That's why the Church urges us to make Lent not only about ourselves, what we eat or don't eat, but about the world around us—not to hide from the broken world but to face it and to do our part to heal it.

## ACT

*Take a step toward spiritual growth.*

Whenever and wherever I have a chance to perform an act of generosity, patience, or kindness, I will respond as Jesus and his first disciples would have.

## PRAY

Lord Jesus Christ, we long to know you in the fullness of your glory as Son of God. But for now we accept your invitation to share the ministry you passed on to your first disciples, caring for our sisters and brothers amid the challenges of everyday life. May we serve you now by serving our neighbors and come to live with you forever in heaven. Amen.

# MONDAY, MARCH 18
## SECOND WEEK OF LENT

BEGIN

*Spend a minute or two in silence. Set aside whatever might hinder your prayer.*

PRAY

Deliver us and pardon our sins for your name's sake.

*~Psalm 79:9b*

LISTEN

*Read Luke 6:36–38.*

Jesus said to his disciples: "Be merciful, just as your Father is merciful."

*~Luke 6:36*

## Mercy Is a Form of Fasting

On December 20, 1943, Franz Stigler was a commercial pilot who had been drafted into the German Luftwaffe. Flying his Messerschmitt over Germany on this day, he came alongside an American B-17, piloted by Second Lt. Charles Brown, that had participated in the bombing of a munitions factory. The B-17 had been beset by fifteen German planes and all but blown to pieces—one member of its crew killed and six wounded.

As Brown tried to coax the wreck back to England on one of its four engines, he saw to the right of his cockpit Stigler making incomprehensible gestures. Brown was sure Stigler was going to finish off the B-17, but the German made no move, and Brown ordered his gunner to fire at the Messerschmitt. Almost simultaneously, Stigler snapped Brown a salute and peeled off, heading back into Germany. Brown brought his plane safely back to England.

Although he was fighting in the service of the Nazi government, Stigler had been schooled in the idea that it is dishonorable to fire on an enemy that is vulnerable. To him, Brown's crew in its B-17, with large parts of it blown away, was in that category.

Stigler and Brown survived the war and found each other in 1990; Stigler explained that, although he was risking a charge of treason, he had been trying to escort the bomber safely out of Germany.

Compassion—demonstrated so dramatically in this incident—is indispensable in a disciple of Jesus, who was compassion itself. If Stigler was merciful in the extraordinary circumstances of war, and at great personal risk, how can we not be merciful in the interactions of our everyday lives? Showing compassion often means giving up pride and self-importance, and that can be as valuable a form of fasting as any other.

ACT

*Take a step toward spiritual growth.*

I will recall someone I have judged harshly—someone I know or someone I have learned about—and take time to consider what part compassion should play in my feelings about this person.

PRAY

Lord Jesus Christ, when a woman was brought to you, accused of a serious sin, your first response was not judgment but compassion. May we who are your disciples always respond in the same way, no matter the sinner or the sin. Amen.

# TUESDAY, MARCH 19
## JOSEPH, HUSBAND OF MARY

BEGIN

*Spend a minute or two in silence. Set aside whatever might hinder your prayer.*

PRAY

The promises of the LORD I will sing forever; through all generations my mouth shall proclaim your faithfulness.

*~Psalm 89:2*

LISTEN

*Read Matthew 1:16, 18–21, 24a.*

The angel of the Lord appeared to Joseph in a dream and said, "Joseph, son of David, do not be afraid to take Mary your wife into your home. For it is through the Holy Spirit that this child has been conceived in her. . . ." When Joseph awoke, he did as the angel of the Lord had commanded him.

*~Matthew 1:20b, 24*

### A Truly Just Man

St. John XXIII made an interesting observation about Joseph, the husband of Mary, and about John the Baptist—namely, that it is reasonable to assume that they ascended into heaven along with Jesus forty days after his Resurrection.

In fact, in a homily delivered on the Solemnity of the Ascension in 1960, the pope said that idea also applied to faithful people who had died before the Resurrection—notably those Jesus reassured of salvation when he "descended into hell," as we proclaim in the Apostles' Creed.

Pope John didn't define this as dogma, but he said that *piamente noi possiamo credere*—we are able to piously believe it. The pope was alluding to the idea that original sin "closed" heaven to the souls of the just who awaited the salvation that would come only with the Resurrection of Jesus.

Joseph, of course, would have been among the just— he was the just man *par excellence*. Despite how important a figure he is in the narrative of our faith, we know little about him. Unlike the effusive John the Baptist, Joseph never even speaks in the gospels. But what we do know about Joseph is what he did in unique circumstances that he could have only dimly understood. He somehow came to know that God wanted him to take the pregnant Mary as his wife. He accepted that calling and remained faithful to it, regardless of the difficulties that likely followed, including the threat to the child's life from Herod the Great.

Joseph did God's will.

We don't know much about him, but what we know is enough. We need only imitate his example, and we will someday join him in the presence of God.

ACT

*Take a step toward spiritual growth.*

I will spend my prayer time today reviewing how I discern what is God's will in the decisions I make in my everyday life.

PRAY

Almighty God, help us to imitate your servant Joseph by being attentive to your word, quietly trying to make our choices in keeping with your divine will. Amen.

# Wednesday, March 20
## Second Week of Lent

BEGIN

*Spend a minute or two in silence. Set aside whatever might hinder your prayer.*

PRAY

But my trust is in you, O Lord; I say, "You are my God." In your hands is my destiny.

*~Psalm 31:15–16a*

LISTEN

*Read Matthew 20:17–28.*

[Jesus] replied, "My chalice you will indeed drink, but to sit at my right and at my left, this is not mine to give but is for those for whom it has been prepared by my Father."

*~Matthew 20:23*

## No Easy Pass to Heaven

I once taught students who had been granted high school diplomas but hadn't mastered English grammar and composition sufficiently to matriculate at community colleges. They had to succeed in a pass/fail course in order to proceed with higher education.

The head of the English department in one of those colleges told me of her frustration with the high schools that had graduated these students without requiring them to master the fundamentals of the language. She was equally frustrated with parents who often harassed her if their sons and daughters were not getting satisfactory grades on tests and essays.

These parents were ambitious in the same way as the mother of the apostles James and John—they wanted their children to reap rewards without enduring the necessary trials. The mother described in today's gospel reading asked Jesus to promise that her boys would have places of honor in his kingdom. Jesus told her sons that he and they would drink of the same cup, meaning that they would take up the difficult and often dangerous vocation of spreading the Gospel in a world that often would not welcome it. They would get no easy pass to heaven.

As disciples of Jesus, we accept the same reality. We may identify ourselves as Christians, receive the sacraments, and attend Mass regularly, but we will fully be disciples of Jesus only if we witness to the Gospel by what we say and what we do every day of our lives.

What this means will be different for each person; the challenge may range from opportunities for small acts of kindness and charity to opportunities for heroism. Either way, we must drink from the same cup that Jesus drank from and meet those opportunities, day after day, as he would have done.

ACT

*Take a step toward spiritual growth.*

I will take time to analyze what being a disciple of Jesus means to me—to what extent it has to do with my destiny and to what extent it has to do with my service to others.

PRAY

Lord Jesus Christ, may I come to eternal life by focusing not on my own desires and ambitions but on the needs of my brothers and sisters. Amen.

# Thursday, March 21
## Second Week of Lent

BEGIN

*Spend a minute or two in silence. Set aside whatever might hinder your prayer.*

PRAY

For the Lord watches over the way of the just, but the way of the wicked vanishes.

*~Psalm 1:6*

LISTEN

*Read Luke 16:19–31.*

Abraham replied, "My child, remember that you received what was good during your lifetime while Lazarus likewise received what was bad; but now he is comforted here, whereas you are tormented."

*~Luke 16:25*

## *Being His Hands and Feet*

For three years, Ginger Sprouse saw an African American man standing or sitting on the same corner in Houston, Texas, in every season and in all kinds of weather. Finally, Ginger, who is white, stopped to talk to him and learned that he was Victor Hubbard, thirty-two years old, homeless, and mentally ill. He told Ginger that his mother had left him at the intersection three years before, and he was waiting there in case she came back.

He didn't ask for anything; in fact, he seemed more concerned about Ginger's well-being than about his own. After that, Ginger talked to Victor every day. When winter came, she and her husband took Victor to their house for the night and eventually decided to make him a permanent part of their family.

Ginger created an online fundraising page and a Facebook page called "This is Victor," and she raised tens of thousands of dollars to address some of Victor's needs. Among other things, she took him to mental-health clinics and got him prescriptions to treat his illness, an eye exam, glasses, and new clothes.

The rich man described in Luke's gospel could have helped a stranger with little effort; Ginger Sprouse went out of her way to help a man she did not know. Jesus told the story of Lazarus to call us to make the kind of choice Ginger made. We may not find a man abandoned on a street corner, but none of us need to look far to find people in need. Why would we get involved? Perhaps for the same reason Ginger did: "God wasn't going to allow me to drive by anymore without finding out why Victor was there. All the glory goes to God for putting us together and allowing me to be his hands and feet!"

ACT

*Take a step toward spiritual growth.*

I will reflect on the times that I have been the hands and feet of God, and I will thank him for giving me the opportunities.

PRAY

Creator God, I wish to act in the spirit of the Gospel when brothers and sisters in need cross my path. Please use my hands and my feet as instruments of your compassion and generosity. Amen.

# Friday, March 22
## Second Week of Lent

BEGIN

*Spend a minute or two in silence. Set aside whatever might hinder your prayer.*

PRAY

Remember the marvels the Lord has done.

*~Psalm 105:5a*

LISTEN

*Read Matthew 21:33–43, 45–46.*

"Finally he sent his son to them, thinking, 'They will respect my son.'"

*~Matthew 21:37*

*We All Are Stewards*

In four decades as a newspaper editor, I fired eleven people. The reasons included excessive absenteeism, conflict of interest, and false reporting.

I remember the number, because firing employees was one of the most distasteful experiences of my life. In most instances, I was fond of the folks I had to discharge, and it didn't make the job easier when the employees told me, as several did, that I was right to let them go— that they had brought it on themselves.

In that sense, they were in the same boat as the tenants Jesus describes in the parable in today's gospel reading. Whatever punishment the absentee owner would impose on "that wicked crowd" would be the result of their own behavior.

The parable of the tenants is often interpreted as a warning to religious leaders that they had failed in their stewardship, that they had rejected and persecuted God's prophets, that they had rejected God's Son, and that they would be ousted and replaced. But there is a broader significance to this story, one that applies to anyone: we are all given stewardship of parts of creation that belong to God—our bodies and health, our families, our communities, and the part of the marketplace where we work or do business. All that we have is leased to us by God, who is generous but who wants something in return.

He doesn't want part of the proceeds; he wants us to be as generous in our care and disposal of our part of creation as he was in giving it to us. He wants us, in using what we have, to think first of the good of others rather than thinking first of our own satisfaction.

It's not too much to say that he wants us to be like God.

ACT

*Take a step toward spiritual growth.*

I will think about the parts of creation that are at my disposal or in my care and consider how I use them for the common good.

PRAY

Eternal God, you have given me life, and you have placed a share of your creation in my care. Help me to use what I have received not only to sustain myself but first to help and comfort others and to build your kingdom on earth. Amen.

# SATURDAY, MARCH 23
## SECOND WEEK OF LENT

BEGIN

*Spend a minute or two in silence. Set aside whatever might hinder your prayer.*

PRAY

He pardons all your iniquities, he heals all your ills.
He redeems your life from destruction.

*~Psalm 103:3–4a*

LISTEN

*Read Luke 15:1–3, 11–32.*

"While he was still a long way off, his father caught sight of him, and was filled with compassion. He ran to his son, embraced him and kissed him."

*~Luke 15:20*

## *One Reason: Mercy*

"'Home is the place where, when you have to go there, / They have to take you in.'

"'I should have called it / Something you somehow haven't to deserve.'"

Those lines, spoken in turn by Mary and Warren, are taken from Robert Frost's poem, "The Death of the Hired Man." A couple is discussing the return of Silas, who often works around the couple's farm but drifts away without warning when Warren needs him most. A debilitated Silas has returned in winter—Mary fears that it's the last time—but Warren is unwilling to accept him. Warren recites the reasons for turning Silas away; Mary does not deny the hired man's shortcomings, acknowledging that "Silas is what he is." She offers only one reason—mercy—for giving the dying man refuge in the only home he knows.

Whether or not Robert Frost intended it, Mary in this poem expresses the kind of unconditional love that is at the heart of the gospel story of the father and his sons. Jesus told that story because he overheard the Pharisees and scribes bemoaning his association with "tax collectors and sinners"—folks who were far more problematic than poor old Silas.

The gospels do not tell us if all of those reprobates reformed under the influence of Jesus, but Jesus didn't take their pasts into account, and he didn't put any preconditions on his willingness to break bread with them—just as the father in the parable didn't wait to hear the litany of his younger son's sins before rushing out to welcome him home.

Jesus calls us to the same level of mercy. If we are to fast from something during Lent, why not fast from any grudge, any hurt, any judgment that keeps us from welcoming someone back into our good graces?

ACT

*Take a step toward spiritual growth.*

In my heart, I will let go of any lingering anger or resentment that I might be clinging to because of perceived wrongs done to me in the past.

PRAY

Lord Jesus Christ, by word and example, you taught us to extend mercy and forgiveness to those who have harmed or slighted us. May we always imitate the father in the parable by being the first to extend the hand of reconciliation. Amen.

# Sunday, March 24
## Third Week of Lent

BEGIN

*Spend a minute or two in silence. Set aside whatever might hinder your prayer.*

PRAY

Merciful and gracious is the L ORD, slow to anger and abounding in kindness.

*~Psalm 103:8*

LISTEN

*Read Luke 13:1–9.*

"Sir, leave it for this year also, and I shall cultivate the ground around it and fertilize it; it may bear fruit in the future."

*~Luke 13:8*

## *The Patient Gardener*

My grandfather, who emigrated from Italy, kept fig trees at our New Jersey home, and each fall he and a neighbor would bury the trees to keep the frost from killing them.

I miss those folks, those trees, that ritual, and that way of life. But one of our daughters and her husband restored a bit of it one Christmas by giving Pat and me two young potted fig trees. We live in a condominium, so there was no question of burying the trees in the winter; instructions I found online advised moving the pots into the garage, protecting the trees from freezing temperatures, giving them a little water once a month, and cautiously reintroducing them to the early spring sunshine. In other words, if we cared for them and were patient, they had a chance of thriving.

I have seen the conversation between the landowner and the gardener, concerning the fig tree, described as a dialogue between God's judgment and God's mercy. Jesus reminds us of divine judgment with his tales of people massacred by the Romans or others killed by a toppling tower—the message being that we do not know how much time we have to conform our lives to God's will. But Jesus counterbalances this warning with the parable of the fig tree—the message being that God is not quick to give up on us and, in fact, has given us over to the care of the gardener—Christ—who patiently cultivates us with his teaching and his example, his Church and the sacraments.

There is urgency in Jesus' message because our lifetimes are, in fact, limited; but there is also encouragement—the promise of the second chance—that should inspire us to be as fruitful as we can in whatever time we have.

## ACT

*Take a step toward spiritual growth.*

I will consider adopting the "Daily Examen" as a way of detecting God's presence in my life and discerning his direction for me. (Visit ignationspirituality.com and click on "Daily Examen.")

## PRAY

God, our Father, you have placed us in the care of your Son, Jesus Christ, who has taught us by word and example how to live in harmony with your divine will. May we reflect each day on what we have learned from Christ and how we apply it in our daily lives. Amen.

# Monday, March 25

## Solemnity of the Annunciation

BEGIN

*Spend a minute or two in silence. Set aside whatever might hinder your prayer.*

PRAY

Sacrifice or oblation you wished not, but ears open to obedience you gave me.

*~Psalm 40:7*

LISTEN

*Read Luke 1:26–38.*

"Nothing will be impossible for God."

*~Luke 1:37*

### Perfect Model of Faith

If the clock on my computer is accurate, it takes less than two minutes to read St. Luke's account of the Virgin Mary's dialogue with the archangel Gabriel. I am guessing that it took much longer than that for the exchange to make its way from "Hail, full of grace" to "May it be done to me according to your word."

The author of the gospel, who recorded this episode using the labor-intensive method available to him in the first century, gave us only the essentials. But the implication of his statements that Mary was "greatly troubled" and that she "pondered what sort of greeting this might be"—before Gabriel had told her the astounding purpose of his visit—is that Mary took some time to come to terms with this experience. Luke's account, which is so familiar to us, is brief, but the reality for Mary cannot have been so compact. There is no way to adequately express—or for us to fully absorb—the enormity of her act of faith in accepting the role assigned to her by God.

It might seem at times that God asks a lot of us: putting the interests of others ahead of our own; forgiving people who have offended us; loving our enemies. But Mary is the perfect model for us precisely because what God asks of us pales in comparison to what he asked of Mary and what she said yes to, no matter how long it took her to accede to her destiny.

The archangel told Mary what God was calling her to. We do not need an angel: we can see what God calls us to by simply looking around at the poor and the sick and the grieving and the lonely and the marginalized who are within arm's length.

ACT

*Take a step toward spiritual growth.*

Spend some time in prayer, and then write a note to yourself in which you identify one call from God to which you have not yet given your yes.

PRAY

Almighty God, may your Holy Spirit open my mind and heart so that I may imitate our Blessed Mother by discerning your call and answering with an unqualified yes. Amen.

# Tuesday, March 26
## Third Week of Lent

BEGIN

*Spend a minute or two in silence. Set aside whatever might hinder your prayer.*

PRAY

Your ways, O LORD, make known to me; teach me your paths.

*~Psalm 25:4*

LISTEN

*Read Matthew 18:21–35.*

Peter approached Jesus and asked him, "Lord, if my brother sins against me, how often must I forgive him? As many as seven times?"

*~Matthew 18:21*

## *I Bear No Grudge*

On November 8, 1987, the Provisional IRA planted a bomb in a town in Northern Ireland, intending to kill police and military personnel during a memorial service for war dead. The bomb detonated early and among the eleven people who died as a result was twenty-year-old Marie Wilson, who was buried under six feet of debris with her father, Gordon, who somehow survived the blast.

In the aftermath of the explosion, Gordon Wilson astounded people around the world by saying, "I bear no ill will. I bear no grudge," noting that angry talk would not restore his daughter. Wilson, who became a prominent peace activist in Northern Ireland, said he would pray for those who planted the bomb, "tonight and every night."

Implied in Wilson's reaction was the answer to Peter's question at the beginning of today's gospel reading. The number in Jesus' answer—"seventy-seven times"—should not be taken literally. Jesus meant, in effect, that we should not try to measure our forgiveness of those who offend us but rather, like Gordon Wilson, forgive them utterly, once and for all.

This is a difficult challenge in interpersonal relationships; many of us are loathe to forgive an offense from a friend, relative, or colleague. It is a challenge of another order of magnitude when the offender is a murderer who snuffed out one or more innocent lives. Forgiveness does not mean condoning an offensive act; it didn't mean that in Gordon Wilson's case. Forgiveness means breaking the cycle of emotional and physical violence, because until that cycle is broken, there can be no peace for individual human beings or for nations.

We have heard it so often that it might sound like a cliché, but there is truth in that lyric: "Let there be peace on earth, and let it begin with me."

ACT

*Take a step toward spiritual growth.*

I will try to let go of any anger or vindictiveness toward people who have committed crimes such as terrorism and genocide and replace those feelings with a prayerful desire for conversion and salvation for even the worst of sinners.

PRAY

Almighty God, may I imitate you by being merciful toward those who offend me and by praying for their salvation. Amen.

# Wednesday, March 27
## Third Week of Lent

### BEGIN

*Spend a minute or two in silence. Set aside whatever might hinder your prayer.*

### PRAY

He sends forth his command to the earth; swiftly runs his word!

*~Psalm 147:15*

### LISTEN

*Read Matthew 5:17–19.*

"But whoever obeys and teaches these commandments will be called greatest in the Kingdom of heaven."

*~Matthew 5:19b*

### Recasting the Law

Title 8.44 of the municipal code in Carmel by the Sea, California, requires a permit to wear shoes with heels more than two inches high with less than a square inch of surface touching the ground. This ordinance was adopted long ago to free the city from liability if a person wearing high heels were injured while walking on streets and other areas deliberately kept rustic in nature—often meaning that streets and sidewalks had uneven surfaces and were not well lit. A person obtaining a permit indemnified the city from responsibility for injuries resulting from a fall. This ordinance made sense when it was adopted, but it is no longer enforced. Although this example is a bit quirky, it is not unusual in principle, because law is a living thing that evolves along with the society it regulates.

That's what's at play when Jesus says that he has come not to abolish the law but to fulfill it. The history of God's covenant with the human race is a history of evolving law, beginning with the mythic prohibition against eating from the tree in Eden. In the story of the Hebrews' odyssey from Egypt to the Promised Land, we read of a complex body of law fashioned to suit a nomadic people surrounded by pagan influences. In Jesus' mission to extend the divine covenant beyond Israel to all people, the laws of the desert and the demands and strictures added by the sages over the centuries were not apropos.

Without abrogating the bedrock principles that characterized the Jewish faith, Jesus recast the whole law into one that emphasized unconditional love of God and of neighbor—"neighbor" meaning anyone but one's self. If we adhere to the law of Jesus, so simply stated, we will not violate any just law.

ACT

*Take a step toward spiritual growth.*

I will spend some time meditating on the Ten Commandments and particularly contemplating how each commandment resonates with Jesus' command to love God and love our neighbors as ourselves.

PRAY

Lord Jesus Christ, may my love be so complete that everything I do is in keeping with the divine will. Amen.

# Thursday, March 28
## Third Week of Lent

BEGIN

*Spend a minute or two in silence. Set aside whatever might hinder your prayer.*

PRAY

Listen to my voice; then I will be your God and you shall be my people.

*~Jeremiah 7:23a*

LISTEN

*Read Luke 11:14–23.*

"Every kingdom divided against itself will be laid waste and house will fall against house."

*~Luke 11:17*

## A House Divided

In 1858, the Illinois Republican Party nominated Abraham Lincoln to run against Democrat Stephen Douglas for a seat in the United States Senate. Lincoln would lose that election, but in response to the nomination he delivered a speech on the controversy over whether slavery should be expanded into the territories.

Lincoln turned to scripture, alluding to Jesus' words recorded in today's gospel reading. "A house divided against itself cannot stand," Lincoln said. "I believe this government cannot endure, permanently half slave and half free."

Slavery was protected by the Constitution, but Lincoln believed that it was morally wrong and should be restricted to the states where it already existed, and that African Americans were human beings who deserved both freedom and citizenship. Douglas disagreed. Lincoln worried in his speech about a "tendency" in public policy to ultimately permit slavery anywhere in the country where one man chose to enslave another.

What could have been the source of that tendency, endorsed by millions of Americans? Many if not most people today, unlike the contemporaries of Jesus, will deny that the devil prompts people to practice or tolerate something as clearly uncivilized as slavery. Pope Francis, on the other hand, has declared that "the devil exists" and has warned against demonic temptations that draw us away from God.

This much is clear: we all experience the temptation, coming from outside ourselves, to act contrary to what we know is God's will, and usually the incentive is our own convenience, profit, comfort, or satisfaction. This might take on the dimensions of American slavery or the Holocaust, or something far less dramatic, such as cheating a customer, stealing from an employer, or neglecting the poor and the sick. Lent is the perfect time to identify those "demons" in our lives and to seek God's help in rejecting them.

ACT

*Take a step toward spiritual growth.*

I will intentionally listen for and reject one voice that calls me to behavior that separates me from Jesus, who said, "whoever is not with me is against me."

PRAY

Dear Jesus, I desire to be your disciple in everything I do and to follow your commandment and example of unselfish love. May my observance of Lent and celebration of your Resurrection strengthen me against the temptation to think first of myself. Amen.

# Friday, March 29
## Third Week of Lent

BEGIN

*Spend a minute or two in silence. Set aside whatever might hinder your prayer.*

PRAY

Straight are the paths of the LORD, in them the just walk, but sinners stumble in them.

*~Hosea 14:9b*

LISTEN

*Read Mark 12:28–34.*

"'Hear, O Israel, the Lord our God is Lord alone.'"

*~Mark 12:29*

*The Greatest Commandment*

I am amused when baseball fans in a Facebook room I frequent argue about who was the greatest player of all time. This dialogue, which usually is all in fun but sometimes gets heated, amuses me, because whether a player was the greatest is a subjective judgment.

The roughly twenty thousand men who have played major league baseball since 1871 performed under widely varying conditions using equipment that has changed over the years and governed by rules that continually evolve. Statistics, which often are all we have to go on, can't establish definitively that an outstanding player of the 1980s was greater than a similarly outstanding player of the 1910s.

That same principle applies to arguments about the greatest tenor and the greatest golfer and the greatest justice of the Supreme Court. In general, it is better to stay away from superlatives such as "greatest"; it can save a lot of hard feelings.

But that principle does not apply to the statement Jesus makes in the discussion recorded in today's gospel reading. Citing two commandments embedded in Jewish religious tradition—love of God and love of neighbor—Jesus tells the righteous scribe, "There is no other commandment greater than these."

Jesus can say that definitively because all of the commandments in the Jewish and Christian faiths flow from these two. Anyone who loves God with the total commitment Jesus cites from the Book of Deuteronomy, anyone who loves others with the selfless attitude Jesus cites from the Book of Leviticus, will not violate particular commandments against such sins as arrogance, envy, greed, and violence.

Just as Jesus demonstrated his consummate love for God and mankind by sacrificing his life on the Cross, we are called to live out the greatest commandments by giving our lives to God and to each other.

ACT

*Take a step toward spiritual growth.*

I will meditate on how my personal interactions have been reflections of God's inexhaustible love for the world.

PRAY

Creator God, may my desire to live in keeping with your will be a blessing to the world around me as my words and deeds reflect your love to everyone I meet. Amen.

# Saturday, March 30
## Third Week of Lent

BEGIN

*Spend a minute or two in silence. Set aside whatever might hinder your prayer.*

PRAY

Have mercy on me, O God, in your goodness; in the greatness of your compassion wipe out my offense.

*~Psalm 51:3*

LISTEN

*Read Luke 18:9–14.*

"The one who humbles himself will be exalted."

*~Luke 18:14b*

### *Boy, You Are Lucky*

I was a chronic altar server.

I served at daily and Sunday Masses, funerals and weddings, novenas, and Stations of the Cross. Many of my friends were members of the parish, and I imagined that my role gave me a certain status.

One day when I was about fourteen, I walked by the church with Bob, a schoolmate who was neither a Catholic nor any other strain of churchgoer. "Hey," he said, "you go to this church, don't you? Could you take me inside?"

I ushered Bob inside, as if I owned the place, and answered the questions of my ignorant friend. Finally, Bob said in a hushed tone, "Boy, you are lucky! You get to come here all the time to pray."

I was not a competent athlete, as Bob was, nor an exceptional student, a good dancer, or a favorite of the girls. But when I donned the cassock and surplice in the sanctuary where others dared not venture, I thought I was as set apart as the math prodigy or the quarterback.

Regular church attendance was commonplace in that era, and I looked askance at folks like Bob. Now, however, I am aware of the parallel between the younger me and the Pharisee in the parable, and I feel that the Holy Spirit has been at work.

I can't recall, verbatim if at all, another remark that a friend made to me when we were fourteen. But Bob's remark has stayed with me for more than sixty years, even though I didn't realize the meaning of it at the time.

Bob had never been in that church before; I was there so much that I probably was a nuisance. But Bob grasped immediately that we should approach God, not with pride and arrogance but with gratitude and humility.

ACT

*Take a step toward spiritual growth.*

I will spend quiet time spontaneously praying to God as a child to a righteous and generous Parent, asking God's forgiveness for my sins and expressing my gratitude for his mercy.

PRAY

Generous Father, may I always be mindful that all I have I owe to you, and may I always approach you as a grateful child, mindful of my frailties but eager to please you. Amen.

# Sunday, March 31
## Fourth Week of Lent

BEGIN

*Spend a minute or two in silence. Set aside whatever might hinder your prayer.*

PRAY

Glorify the LORD with me, let us together extol his name.

*~Psalm 34:4*

LISTEN

*Read Luke 15:1–3, 11–32.*

"But now we must celebrate and rejoice, because your brother was dead and has come to life again; he was lost and has been found."

*~Luke 15:32*

*Why Do Men Fight?*

James Longstreet was one of the leading Confederate generals in the Civil War. In that role, he was at odds with an old friend, Ulysses S. Grant, the key military figure in the Union victory. Grant rejected every premise on which officers—including former colleagues—had joined the Confederacy. He was aggressive in his campaigns to defeat the armies led by these old comrades.

When Confederate general Robert E. Lee realized that he did not have the resources to continue, he surrendered his army, effectively ending the war. Longstreet went to see Grant, who was in a house in Appomattox Courthouse, Virginia, waiting for Lee to sign the terms of surrender. In his eponymous biography of Grant, Ron Chernow reports that when Grant saw Longstreet enter the house, "he sprang to his feet, shook his hand, offered him a cigar, and invited him to play brag, the card game they had enjoyed before the war."

Later, in an interview with the *New York Times*, Longstreet recalled Grant's generosity: "Great God, thought I to myself, how my heart swells out to such a magnanimous touch of humanity! Why do men fight who were born to be brothers?"

Grant could have shunned Longstreet; he also could have argued that men like Longstreet should be tried, imprisoned, even executed. But Grant chose not to contribute to a cycle of vengeance and violence; he chose instead the blessings of common humanity. Grant chose, on the grand scale of a war that cost about seven hundred thousand lives, what the father in the parable chose on the scale of family relationships.

The lesson for us is plain. In all of our encounters with those born to be our brothers and sisters, we are called to choose the same mercy that God offers to us.

ACT

*Take a step toward spiritual growth.*

I will resolve in prayer always to distinguish between justice and revenge and always to be willing to heal my relationship with someone who has wronged me.

PRAY

Lord Jesus, you teach us to be the initiators of peace when others have injured us. May we put this lesson into practice by putting aside pride and welcoming without condescension or bitterness those who want to reconcile with us. Amen.

# MONDAY, APRIL 1
## FOURTH WEEK OF LENT

BEGIN

*Spend a minute or two in silence. Set aside whatever might hinder your prayer.*

PRAY

Seek good and not evil so that you may live, and the LORD will be with you.

*~Amos 5:14*

LISTEN

*Read John 4:43–54.*

"Unless you people see signs and wonders, you will not believe."

*~John 4:48*

## *Imitation of Christ*

There are several versions of the story of a man who went for a walk in the woods and realized at dusk that he was lost. "Dear God," he prayed, "I am not religious, but if you get me out of these woods, I will go to church, obey your commandments, and just become a better person." As he concluded this prayer, he spotted a sign pointing the way out of the woods, so he quickly added, "Never mind, God, I found it myself."

That story evokes the cliché that "there are no atheists in a foxhole," meaning that some people turn to God only in times of trouble. And both the story and the cliché come to mind in connection with the gospel passage about the royal official whose son was mortally ill and who begged Jesus to heal the child. Some of Jesus' contemporaries were interested in him only because he could heal the blind and deaf, cure the sick, and calm the sea. They did not take seriously his teaching of humble piety and selfless love of all other people.

It seems that Jesus tries at first to determine whether the royal official is a foxhole convert, and Jesus' willingness to heal the child—besides being consistent with his compassionate nature—suggests a confidence that the worried father is more than an opportunist. But the fact that Jesus healed the boy should not distract us from the reason for his initial reaction to the father's request. Faith in Jesus does not mean faith in a wonder worker who might dazzle us or bail us out; faith in Jesus means commitment to the kind of life he lived and preached—a life in which we imitate him in mercy, generosity, and justice, even when things don't go our way.

ACT

*Take a step toward spiritual growth.*

I will resolve not to be discouraged or weakened in faith if things I pray for do not come to pass.

PRAY

Good and gracious God, you have given us stewardship over your creation, and you have given us free will so that we may contribute to our own destiny. Help us to remain faithful to you as we use our human resources to meet the difficulties and challenges that are sure to arise in life. Amen.

# Tuesday, April 2
## Fourth Week of Lent

BEGIN

*Spend a minute or two in silence. Set aside whatever might hinder your prayer.*

PRAY

A clean heart create for me, O God; give me back the joy of your salvation.

*~Psalm 51:12a, 14a*

LISTEN

*Read John 5:1–16.*

"Look, you are well; do not sin any more."

*~John 5:14b*

## *To Begin Anew*

The dialogue with the paralyzed man, described in today's gospel reading, is one of the most curious of Jesus' conversations. Jesus' remark after the cure is noticeably harsh: "Look, you are well; do not sin any more, so that nothing worse may happen to you."

Compare that to Jesus' patient comment to the woman accused of adultery: "Woman, where did they all disappear to? Has no one condemned you?" "No one, sir," she answered. Jesus said, "Nor do I condemn you. You may go. But from now on, avoid this sin" (see John 8:10b–11).

It might appear that by warning of "something worse" Jesus is connecting the man's disability and his unspecified sins, which Jesus seems to know all about. But we know that Jesus rejected the common idea that illness or disability was punishment for sin. So it seems, rather, that Jesus is suggesting that this man should take the opportunity, signaled by his cure, to begin life fresh and cease behavior that might cause him trouble far worse than paralysis.

Many commentators infer that the paralyzed man never made the effort to find a cure—that it was easier for him to blame someone else for his troubles. That implication and Jesus' inference that the man is a habitual sinner don't create a positive image of a fellow who at first blush seemed like a sympathetic character. Of course, we don't know what that man did after his second conversation with Jesus; perhaps he reformed and became a pious Jew and an exemplary citizen.

What matters to us are two lessons we can derive from his story that are particularly appropriate to Lent: we must take responsibility for the choices we make in life, and we should accept the opportunities that God offers us, repeatedly, to put our sins behind us and begin life anew.

## ACT

*Take a step toward spiritual growth.*

I will pray about what I would bring to the Lord if I were to receive the sacrament of Reconciliation today and about the particular ways in which I would like to start life anew.

## PRAY

Lord Jesus, you have taught us that God forgives anyone who comes to him in penance. May we have the humility to acknowledge our sins and the determination to rise to new life, renewed by the grace you earned for us. Amen.

# Wednesday, April 3
## Fourth Week of Lent

BEGIN

*Spend a minute or two in silence. Set aside whatever might hinder your prayer.*

PRAY

The LORD is near to all who call upon him, to all who call upon him in truth.

*~Psalm 145:18*

LISTEN

*Read John 5:17–30.*

"Whoever does not honor the Son does not honor the Father who sent him."

*~John 5:23b*

*No Strange Gods*

In 1973, John Lahr published a novel, *The Autograph Hound*, that painted a disturbing picture of a man obsessed with celebrities. The title character satisfied his fixation through an elaborate collection of autographs. Collecting autographs in itself is a harmless pastime, but in this case it was symptomatic of a disorder in which a person attributed to athletes, entertainers, political figures—indeed, anyone whose name was known to the public—an importance that they do not have. The result was that the man had no identity of his own. Fortunately, few people are fascinated with celebrities to the pathological degree described in Lahr's book, although three prominent actors who read the book told me that it describes a real phenomenon.

In the first commandment, God admonishes us, "You shall not have strange gods before me." The ancient Hebrews knew that commandment to mean that they must not worship the gods of the pagan nations that surrounded them in the Near East. But the commandment was meant for all time, and in the twenty-first century we understand it to mean that no person or possession must take the place of God as the primary focus of our lives. And that does mean that we should not allow our preoccupation with celebrities to distort the values by which we make judgments about our place in the world.

In the discourse in today's gospel passage, Jesus makes it clear that the only Being whose judgment and will ultimately matter in the world, and in each of our lives, is God. Many of those who heard and saw Jesus in his human flesh and blood admired and respected him, but his mission was to fix their attention, and our attention, on the Creator God and to mold their lives according to his will alone.

ACT

*Take a step toward spiritual growth.*

I will review who or what preoccupied me today and ask myself whether I gave God and his will the attention due to them.

PRAY

Almighty God, you are the focal point of our lives, the source of truth, the guide to righteousness. May we never allow any person or possession to occupy the place that properly belongs to you. Amen.

# Thursday, April 4
## Fourth Week of Lent

BEGIN

*Spend a minute or two in silence. Set aside whatever might hinder your prayer.*

PRAY

God so loved the world that he gave his only-begotten Son, so that everyone who believes in him might have eternal life.

*~John 3:16*

LISTEN

*Read John 5:31–47.*

"The works that the Father gave me to accomplish, these works that I perform testify on my behalf that the Father has sent me."

*~John 5:36b*

## The Highest Authority

One lesson I learned early in my career as a supervisor in the newspaper business was not to rely only on the references provided by a job applicant but to also try to get input from employers the applicant didn't mention. This can be a time-consuming process; employers who worry about repercussions from a negative review often are willing to provide only confirmation of the years of employment. And even when I could get testimony from additional sources, I had to carefully weigh the credibility of those sources and their comments.

The implication of today's gospel passage is that references were not an issue where Jesus was concerned. His critics often questioned his authority to teach and to heal. In response he could point to impeccable credentials: the prophecies in Hebrew Scriptures, the testimony of John the Baptist, and the endorsement of the ultimate source—God the Father.

All of this was clear to those who became the first disciples of Jesus, but it eluded those who did not want to acknowledge the validity of his ministry. Why did these latter reject what others embraced? There probably were multiple reasons. Some may have been defending their own status in the religious community. Some may have been jealous of Jesus, who was attracting the respect and affection of many Jews and Gentiles. And most significantly, some may have found it more convenient to follow the status quo than to re-form their lives in keeping with Jesus' challenging message of unconditional love, including love of one's enemies.

By identifying ourselves as Christians, we have recognized that Jesus teaches with the highest authority possible—divine authority. And because we recognize his "credentials" we can hardly help but try as hard and as persistently as possible to apply his teachings of justice, mercy, and love to every aspect of our daily lives.

## ACT

*Take a step toward spiritual growth.*

I will prayerfully read the section of Jesus' Sermon on the Mount contained in the Gospel of Matthew 5:21–48, and apply these lessons to my own life.

## PRAY

Lord Jesus, you taught us, through word and example, to build the kingdom of God on earth through love, justice, and compassion. We receive your teaching as reflecting the will of God. May we always live accordingly. Amen.

# Friday, April 5
## Fourth Week of Lent

BEGIN

*Spend a minute or two in silence. Set aside whatever might hinder your prayer.*

PRAY

The LORD redeems the lives of his servants; no one incurs guilt who takes refuge in him.

*~Psalm 34:23*

LISTEN

*Read John 7:1–2, 10, 25–30.*

"I did not come on my own, but the one who sent me, whom you do not know, is true. I know him, because I am from him, and he sent me."

*~John 7:28b–29*

### An Inconvenient Presence

The campaign for African American civil rights was advanced by images, broadcast throughout the country, of African American citizens being assaulted with dogs, clubs, and fire hoses. Many Americans to whom racial discrimination had been an abstract idea were outraged by the sight of people, who were not only innocent but also in the right, being brutalized by agencies that should have been protecting them.

In a similar way, although we have often read today's gospel passage and others like it, we should be horrified by the matter-of-fact statements that some of Jesus' countrymen wanted to kill him. There is an astounding paradox in that fact: people wanted to kill a man whose message was love of God and neighbor, forgiveness of enemies, and compassion for the disadvantaged.

Unfortunately, this sentiment persists today, only in another form. While the glorified Jesus cannot be murdered again, there are many people who want to snuff out his influence in the world through ridicule, contempt, and even violence directed at his followers. Jesus is the target of those who profit from the spread of secularism and individualism, deniers of fundamental truth, and adherents to religious extremism. He is also an inconvenient presence to those who want to pursue lives of self-satisfaction as though there were no universal morality.

We who profess to be his disciples cannot ignore the vehemence directed at his person and his teaching. We cannot be embarrassed to let others know that we worship God, that we experience God in the person of Jesus Christ, and that we live according to his Gospel. We are called to be his missionary disciples, meaning that we not only profess to be his followers but also bear witness to his message, letting the world know, to paraphrase St. Paul, that Christ lives in us.

## A C T

*Take a step toward spiritual growth.*

I will take advantage of any opportunity to share my Christian faith, unapologetically and without embarrassment.

## P R A Y

Lord Jesus Christ, you preached and practiced peace in a world bristling with hate and violence. May we always be sources of peace in what we say and in how we live. Amen.

# Saturday, April 6
## Fourth Week of Lent

BEGIN

*Spend a minute or two in silence. Set aside whatever might hinder your prayer.*

PRAY

Blessed are they who have kept the word with a generous heart and yield a harvest through perseverance.

*~Luke 8:15*

LISTEN

*Read John 7:40–53.*

Some in the crowd who heard these words of Jesus said, "This is truly the Prophet."
    Others said, "This is the Christ."

*~John 7:40–41a*

## Listen to Him

Today's gospel reading is unusual in that it is about Jesus but Jesus is not present in the scene. Instead, the passage consists of comments made by people who have just heard him speak: the temple guards, the chief priests and the Pharisees, and Nicodemus, who paid clandestine visits to Jesus. The dialogue turns into arguments, first among "the crowd" and then between the Pharisees and Nicodemus.

The Pharisees, who perhaps don't know where Jesus was born, cling to the argument that he cannot be the Messiah both because scripture says that the Messiah will come from Bethlehem and because the Pharisees look down their noses at Galilee—where Jesus spent his childhood—because many Gentiles lived in that region.

But the guards and Nicodemus make a salient point that has to do not with where Jesus came from but with what Jesus said. "Never before has anyone spoken like this man," say the guards. "Does our law condemn a man before it first hears him?" asks Nicodemus. These conversations in Jesus' absence remind us that to know Jesus is to listen to what he has said.

There has always been a lot of speculation about matters concerning Jesus that are not discussed in the gospels. In ancient times, this speculation led some authors to write "gospels" of their own. In modern times there are periodic efforts to discover the "historical Jesus."

But to find Jesus, we need look no further than his words preserved in the canonical gospels. And while we hear short excerpts from those gospels when we attend Mass, we can get to know Jesus even better if we read the gospels more thoroughly on our own.

After all, God the Father told us, "This is my beloved Son. Listen to him."

## A C T

*Take a step toward spiritual growth.*

I will choose one of the gospels and prayerfully read it over time, contemplating its meaning in my daily life.

## P R A Y

Lord Jesus Christ, we praise you and thank you for your teaching that has been preserved for us in the gospels. We cherish all that you have said, because you have the words of everlasting life. Amen.

# SUNDAY, APRIL 7
## FIFTH WEEK OF LENT

BEGIN

*Spend a minute or two in silence. Set aside whatever might hinder your prayer.*

PRAY

Remember not the events of the past, the things of long ago consider not; see, I am doing something new!

*~Isaiah 43:18–19a*

LISTEN

*Read John 8:1–11.*

"Let the one among you who is without sin be the first to throw a stone at her." . . . And in response, they went away one by one.

*~John 8:7a, 9a*

## *Hatred Transformed to Love*

Joe Bednarsky rose so high in the ranks of the Ku Klux Klan that his robe was purple rather than the mundane white worn by the rank and file. He marched in Klan rallies around the country, burned crosses, insulted African American people, and once used a slingshot to wound an African American woman who was holding a baby at the time. He went to jail for that attack. Bednarsky has said that he realized in 2005 that God was calling him to change his ways, but he found it difficult to give up the aspects of Klan life that boosted his fragile ego.

He finally quit the Klan in 2007. In 2009, Bednarsky started taking meals at a soup kitchen at the Bethel AME

Church in Millville, New Jersey. Being white, six foot six, and 330 pounds, Bednarsky stood out in the crowd.

Initially, the pastor and the congregation were suspicious of him, but his relationship with the Rev. Charles E. Wilkins Sr. developed to the point that Bednarsky took on the responsibility of protecting the church and the pastor personally. Wilkins has said that some people in the congregation have had a hard time forgiving Bednarsky for his past life. But as extraordinary as it would be for them to forgive a man who once hated them, it is exactly what Jesus calls us to.

Ours is a faith of optimism, not of pessimism, as today's gospel reading dramatizes. Jesus declined to condemn the adulterous woman without even hearing her repent; he simply told her to sin no more.

This is why the Church invites us to observe the season of Lent—so that we can turn to God in repentance with confidence that he will forgive us anything and so that we can resolve to extend the same generosity to each other.

### ACT

*Take a step toward spiritual growth.*

I will receive the sacrament of Reconciliation and forgive, in prayer, anyone who has offended me.

### PRAY

Lord Jesus Christ, you taught us to ask God in prayer to "forgive us our trespasses as we forgive those who trespass against us." We have faith that God will forgive us when we come to him in penance. May we have the openness of heart to be as generous with those who have offended us in any way, forgiving them even as you forgave your persecutors. Amen.

# MONDAY, APRIL 8
## FIFTH WEEK OF LENT

BEGIN

*Spend a minute or two in silence. Set aside whatever might hinder your prayer.*

PRAY

He guides me in right paths for his name's sake.

*~Psalm 23:3b*

LISTEN

*Read John 8:12–20.*

"I testify on my behalf and so does the Father who sent me."

*~John 8:18*

### Which Side Are You On?

One blessing of working at a local newspaper was the opportunity to interact with people who regarded the news staff as friends. Some of these people were helpful, and some just needed someone to talk to.

One woman, who lived in a nearby apartment, would call the newsroom almost every night to chat with reporters and editors she had come to know on a first-name basis. She wasn't just anyone. She was the Grand Duchess Anastasia, daughter of Nicholas II, the last tsar of Russia. Or so she said. Whoever answered the phone that night would let her talk and have that human connection she seemed to crave. Occasionally a small group getting off duty at about 2 a.m. would visit her and share drinks and smokes. They knew she wasn't Anastasia, but to tell her that would only have hurt her feelings; in the relationship she had with those news folks, it didn't matter.

But it's not that way with Jesus and the claim he made, recorded in today's gospel passage and elsewhere in scripture. He said he was God's own Son. He said that to know him was to know the Father. He went to his physical death making this claim.

In our society, infused with secularism, some people who would be embarrassed to dismiss Jesus altogether claim to respect him as a teacher and a prophet and even as a role model.

No. That's not what Jesus said, and what he said was radical.

What he said draws a line that asks, which side are you on? We either accept Jesus' claim that he is the "light of the world" or we do not. And if we do, we bind ourselves to him, live according to his word, and reflect his light on the world around us.

ACT

*Take a step toward spiritual growth.*

I will intentionally remember the divinity of Jesus Christ whenever I become aware of creation around me and aware of the gift of my own life, and I will pray, "My Lord and my God."

PRAY

Lord Jesus Christ, we believe that you are the Son, the second person of the Blessed Trinity, one with the Father and the Holy Spirit, and that you are the Savior foretold by the prophets. May our faith in you inspire us to live by your word and your example of mercy, love, and justice. Amen.

# Tuesday, April 9
## Fifth Week of Lent

BEGIN

*Spend a minute or two in silence. Set aside whatever might hinder your prayer.*

PRAY

The nations shall revere your name, O Lord, and all the kings of the earth your glory.

*~Psalm 102:16*

LISTEN

*Read John 8:21–30.*

"The one who sent me is true, and what I heard from him I tell the world."

*~John 8:26b*

## *They Did Not Know Him*

Two bird-watchers patronizing a restaurant with a tropical theme paused on their way out for a critical look at a parrot on a perch. They discussed the flaws in the taxidermy and agreed that the parrot was the work of an amateur. As they turned away, the parrot said, "Thank you! Please come again." It was a case of people who were ostensibly experts failing to recognize the real thing when it was under their noses.

That was the situation of the Pharisees described in today's gospel reading. They had become so rigid in their understanding of their religious tradition that they did not recognize the fulfilment of its promise, even when the embodiment of that promise was revealing himself to them. Jesus in this passage twice refers to himself with the expression "I AM," alluding to the answer Moses received when he asked for God's name: "I AM." But the Pharisees, who can recite the lines from the book of Exodus in which God gives that response, don't understand what Jesus is saying, just as they don't understand Jesus' predictions of his death, all because they can't break away from their preconceived view of God and the world.

By now, these Pharisees also know what Jesus has been doing—comforting the poor, healing the sick and the disabled, encouraging fidelity to God and his commandments. But when Jesus says that he does only what is pleasing to God, the Pharisees again do not understand.

Perhaps we have an advantage over the Pharisees in that we already acknowledge that Jesus is both human and divine, the Son of God. But we are not his disciples only because we intellectually acknowledge who he is. Our discipleship consists of truthfully saying with him: I always do what is pleasing to God.

## ACT

*Take a step toward spiritual growth.*

I will review the ministries of my parish, asking myself if they offer me an opportunity to do what is pleasing to God. If I am already active in parish ministries, I will invite a less active parishioner to join me.

## PRAY

Lord Jesus Christ, everything you said and did in your ministry on earth was from God. May we model our lives according to your words and deeds so that whatever we do or say will be pleasing to God. Amen.

# Wednesday, April 10
## Fifth Week of Lent

*Spend a minute or two in silence. Set aside whatever might hinder your prayer.*

PRAY

Blessed are you in the firmament of heaven, praise-worthy and glorious forever.

*~Daniel 3:56*

LISTEN

*Read John 8:31–42.*

"If you remain in my word, you will truly be my disciples, and you will know the truth, and the truth will set you free."

*~John 8:31b*

## A God of Joy

It's a tradition in twelve-step programs for a person who introduces him or herself to a group to add, "and I am an alcoholic." As I understand it, a person doesn't make this declaration as a form of self-deprecation. Rather, stating the truth in this manner frees a person from the denial and sense of shame that would be obstacles to healing. A person can't be treated for a disease unless the disease has been diagnosed. Alcoholism is a disease; it has to be named before it can be treated.

This is an example of truth being the key to freedom, a principle Jesus sets forth in today's gospel passage—one of the most frequently quoted statements in the Bible. Jesus was telling people that becoming his disciples would free them to let go of interpretations of their religious tradition that were suffocating them.

The truth that Jesus offered was that God's covenant with Israel was being renewed and extended to the whole human race; the focus of the new covenant was not guilt or sacrifice or condemnation but reconciliation, charity, justice, and forgiveness. In this new covenant, people would encounter God neither in a burning bush nor in a pillar of fire or smoke nor in a secluded sanctuary that only a priest could enter but in the person of Jesus Christ, in whom God and humanity were both present. In this covenant, in other words, God and his people would literally embrace, and people would be free to express their faith in a God of joy, not a God of fear.

That's why Christian faith is not morbid but exuberant, because it does not end in the confines of the tomb but in the freedom of our Savior as he breaks forever the bonds of sin and death.

## ACT

*Take a step toward spiritual growth.*

I will intentionally seek a gentle way to share with a friend who has been away from the Church the freedom and joy I experience through my relationship with God in Jesus Christ.

## PRAY

Jesus Christ, our Savior, we thank you for the freedom we have gained because of your triumph over sin and death. While worldly forces seek to confine us in habits born of selfishness and hardness of heart, may we always choose instead the joy that comes only from loving you and keeping your word. Amen.

# Thursday, April 11
## Fifth Week of Lent

BEGIN

*Spend a minute or two in silence. Set aside whatever might hinder your prayer.*

PRAY

Look to the LORD in his strength; seek to serve him constantly.

*~Psalm 105:4*

LISTEN

*Read John 8:51–59.*

"Amen, amen, I say to you, whoever keeps my word will never see death."

*~John 8:51*

*Woe to the Stony Hearts*

When I was an altar server, one of my assignments was to rush through the church with a colleague while the Gloria was sung at the Easter Vigil and remove the veils from the sacred images, including the most important image—the crucifix over the altar.

Some commentators associate the veiling of sacred images with the last line of today's gospel reading: "Jesus hid and went out of the temple area." It is a melancholy thing to contemplate—that Jesus offers people a path to salvation, to a new, intimate relationship with God, and they respond by trying to stone him.

This is not the only time we read in the gospels that Jesus escaped from an angry mob. St. Luke records that Jesus also did that at the beginning of his public ministry, when people in his hometown of Nazareth turned against him after he proclaimed in the synagogue that he was the anointed one described in Isaiah's prophesy.

Concerning the incident described in the Gospel of John, St. Augustine wrote, "As a man he fled from the stones, but woe to them from whose stony hearts God flies away." The veiling of the crucifix reminds us of this: the worst possible tragedy of a person's life is to be separated from God. We see that imagery in the book of Genesis when God exiles Adam and Eve from the Garden of Eden, and from his presence. Indeed, the horror of hell is not fire but the eternal absence of God.

And so, as we review our lives during Lent, we don't focus so much on an action that breached this or that moral rule but rather on our willingness to even momentarily separate ourselves from God as well as on the sure way—repentance—to restore ourselves to his friendship.

## ACT

*Take a step toward spiritual growth.*

I will spend quiet time contemplating the peace that comes from the presence of God in my life and the anticipation of life forever with him.

## PRAY

"An Act of Spiritual Communion"
My Jesus, I believe that you are present in the Most Holy Sacrament. I love you above all things, and I desire to receive you into my soul. Since I cannot at this moment receive you sacramentally, come at least spiritually into my heart. I embrace you as if you were already there and unite myself wholly to you. Never permit me to be separated from you. Amen.

*~Attributed to St. Alphonsus Liguori*

# Friday, April 12
## Fifth Week of Lent

BEGIN

*Spend a minute or two in silence. Set aside whatever might hinder your prayer.*

PRAY

I love you, O Lord, my strength, O Lord, my rock, my fortress, my deliverer.

*~Psalm 18:2–3a*

LISTEN

*Read John 10:31–42.*

"If I do not perform my Father's works, do not believe me; but if I perform them, even if you do not believe me, believe the works, so that you may realize and understand that the Father is in me and I am in the Father."

*~John 10:37–38*

## To Do What Jesus Did

Shirley Jackson, a celebrated writer of the twentieth century, published a short story, "The Lottery," in 1948, which described a ritual in which the residents of a small town once a year stoned to death a neighbor who was chosen by lot. "The Lottery" touched themes that included scapegoating and mob psychology. This story, although it was fiction, caused many readers to cancel their subscriptions to *The New Yorker,* which had first published it. Some readers couldn't stomach the idea that otherwise ordinary people would stone to death a person who had done nothing wrong.

How much more outrageous is the true story, related in today's gospel passage, of otherwise ordinary people who would stone a man who had performed many acts of compassion with power that could have come only from God? Those folks couldn't make the connection between the works that Jesus had done in their midst and his declaration that he was the Son of God.

The gospels suggest that Jesus carefully orchestrated his ministry so that his acts of compassion and mercy would prepare people for the eventual revelation that he was not only a human being but also a divine Person, one with God. Some of his contemporaries responded, as we read in this passage ("many there began to believe in him"), and some did not.

Our situation is very different from that of the people who would have stoned Jesus. We abhor such an idea, and we revere Jesus as our Savior and as the Son of God. But there still is the issue of his works, which he said his disciples would imitate. Besides the questions we may ask ourselves during Lent about mistakes we have made, it is fitting to ask how well we have imitated Jesus in bringing love and mercy to our neighbors.

ACT

*Take a step toward spiritual growth.*

I will perform an act in imitation of the "works" of Jesus, perhaps a letter, a phone call, or a visit that I have been neglecting and that would bring comfort or peace to someone I know.

PRAY

Lord Jesus, may we be truly your disciples and continue your ministry through works that mirror your acts of healing and mercy. May we love our brothers and sisters, no matter who they are, as you have loved us. Amen.

# Saturday, April 13
## Fifth Week of Lent

BEGIN

*Spend a minute or two in silence. Set aside whatever might hinder your prayer.*

PRAY

Hear the word of the LORD, O nations, proclaim it on distant isles, and say: He who scattered Israel, now gathers them together.

*~Jeremiah 31:10*

LISTEN

*Read John 11:45–56.*

"What are we going to do? This man is performing many signs. If we leave him alone, all will believe in him, and the Romans will come and take away both our land and our nation."

*~John 11:47b–48*

## Called to Change the World

The other day, an acquaintance of mine was explaining, in a conversation on Facebook, why she doesn't believe in Jesus Christ. She made arguments from history, from science, and from what she regarded as logic. She didn't try to account for the fact that a "nonexistent" person became the axis on which human history has turned, that a handful of people who did believe in him spread his teachings through the known world in a matter of decades, or that more than two billion people identify with him today. She didn't explain why she felt compelled to deny so vigorously that Jesus ever existed. And she didn't say anything about his moral teaching or how it squares with her own values. Better to kill him by denying he existed, I guess, than to confront the transforming challenge he presented—the challenge to be sources of new life in the world through unconditional love.

The critics of Jesus, including the priests and Pharisees presented in today's gospel reading, never address that challenge either. Instead, they worry out loud that Jesus, who presents no threat to the Roman occupiers and doesn't seem to have attracted their attention, will provoke some kind of reprisal. And they worry, too, that his works—such as the raising of Lazarus, alluded to at the beginning of today's gospel reading—and his compelling words will undermine their authority and their influence.

The disciples of Jesus, by contrast, hear in his words a call from God to change the world by following God's own example of unconditional and creative love, without which we, with our immortal souls, would not exist. This is the unique message of Jesus, who is the Word of God, and one cannot dismiss him without hearing what he says and answering yes or no.

ACT

*Take a step toward spiritual growth.*

I will write down the words of Jesus in John 13:34–35 and read them as often as I can today, saying yes in my heart to the Word of God.

PRAY

Lord, Jesus Christ, I believe that you are the Son of God, the Word made flesh, and that you teach the only path to peace on earth. Amen.

# Sunday, April 14
## Palm Sunday of the Lord's Passion

BEGIN

*Spend a minute or two in silence. Set aside whatever might hinder your prayer.*

PRAY

I will proclaim your name to my brethren; in the midst of the assembly I will praise you.

*~Psalm 22:23*

LISTEN

*Read Luke 19:28–40.*

Some of the Pharisees in the crowd said to him, "Teacher, rebuke your disciples." He said in reply, "I tell you, if they keep silent, the stones will cry out!"

*~Luke 19:39–40*

## Discipleship Is Witness

In 1976, I was about to go into Yankee Stadium for a game when I was stopped by Jonathan Kwitny, a reporter for the *Wall Street Journal.* Jon picked me out of the crowd because he and I had worked together in the 1960s. He said the *Journal* had assigned him to interview Yankee fans, who were turning out that season in numbers that hadn't been seen since 1950; in '76 the Yankees were destined to win the pennant for the first time in eleven years, and Jon's assignment was to ask the fans where they had been for the past decade.

Well, that is human nature—support the winner, abandon the loser—and we often hear that tendency invoked in commentaries on the events we commemorate on this Sunday, the triumphal entry into Jerusalem and the trial before Pontius Pilate. However, it is possible to be too glib about that; the gospel doesn't state that the crowd that accompanied Jesus into the holy city with waving branches and shouts of "Hosanna" was identical with the crowd that five days later would demand that Pilate "crucify him!" Perhaps it is more realistic to speculate that some were the same people, some of those in the crowd before Pilate had always been either indifferent or antagonistic toward Jesus, and some of those who shouted his praises on Sunday were hiding in the shadows on Friday. We don't know.

What is more important to us is our own faithfulness. We are called to worship, and we are called to charity, but we are also called to witness. Let us pray today that when Jesus is ignored or dismissed, as he so often is in our time, that we will have the courage to stand with him and be known as his disciples.

## ACT

*Take a step toward spiritual growth.*

Without proselytizing, I will not hesitate in the company of others to attribute my ideals to my faith in Jesus Christ.

## PRAY

Lord Jesus, you never wavered in your love for us, even to the point of dying on the Cross. May we now be faithful to you, proclaiming with our lips and our lives your Gospel of love. Amen.

# Monday, April 15
## Holy Week

BEGIN

*Spend a minute or two in silence. Set aside whatever might hinder your prayer.*

PRAY

Wait for the LORD with courage; be stouthearted, and wait for the LORD.

*~Psalm 27:14*

LISTEN

*Read John 12:1–11.*

"You always have the poor with you, but you do not always have me."

*~John 12:8*

## In Giving We Receive

"The Iscariot," as the author calls him, was probably exaggerating when he said the oil Mary used to anoint Jesus was worth three hundred days' wages. Judas no doubt was using the Middle Eastern technique of overstatement to emphasize his point that the oil was very costly. Jesus' reply, as reported in the Gospel of Matthew (26:13), was, "Wherever this gospel is proclaimed in the whole world, what she has done will be spoken of, in memory of her."

And here we are, twenty-one centuries later, speaking of it.

Why is that? Was Jesus insensitive to the plight of the poor and also tolerant of waste? With respect to the poor, we know the answer. His expectation that his disciples would help the least of his brothers and sisters was central to his teaching. With respect to waste, we can infer the answer from the fact that in the episodes in which he miraculously fed thousands, he instructed the apostles to collect the leftovers—and I think we can infer from Jesus' character in general that he would not want food or any other useful commodity wasted.

More likely, Jesus thought Mary's act was memorable because the use of that expensive oil dramatized how completely she had given herself over as his disciple. The Church remembers it because that's also what Jesus expects of us: total, self-emptying commitment, which we express by caring for the needs of others, even if that means letting go of some luxuries that benefit no one but ourselves.

That's why the modern Church emphasizes charity even more than fasting during Lent, because "it is in giving that we receive and in dying that we are born to eternal life."

ACT

*Take a step toward spiritual growth.*

I will contemplate in prayer how I may have held back in my commitment as a missionary disciple of Jesus. I will consider what part of my life I am ready to surrender in his service.

PRAY

Take, O Lord, and receive my entire liberty, my memory, my understanding, and my whole will. All that I am, all that I have, you have given me, and I will give it back again to you to be disposed of according to your good pleasure. Amen.

*~St. Ignatius Loyola*

# Tuesday, April 16
## Holy Week

BEGIN

*Spend a minute or two in silence. Set aside whatever might hinder your prayer.*

PRAY

In your justice rescue me, and deliver me; incline your ear to me, and save me.

*~Psalm 71:2*

LISTEN

*Read John 13:21–33, 36–38.*

"Now is the Son of Man glorified, and God is glorified in him."

*~John 13:31b*

### Eager to Forgive

John Anthony Walker, a US naval officer, negotiated a job as a spy for the Soviet Union in order to deal with his financial problems. Besides betraying his own country, he made a plea bargain with federal prosecutors in 1985, gaining a lighter sentence for his son and co-conspirator, Michael Walker, by testifying against another officer involved in the ring. In terms of the military information the Soviets obtained through John Walker's connivance, this was one of the most damaging episodes of its kind in history.

Incidents in which a person conspires against those who trusted him are uniquely hurtful and, in their own way, sad. That sadness permeates the drama that unfolds in today's gospel passage as Judas turns on Jesus and Jesus predicts that Peter will do the same.

But notice that Jesus did not react to this treachery in a way that would perhaps be more typical of human nature. Jesus anticipated Judas's defection before the apostles assembled for this Passover meal, but he did not ask Judas to stay away. On the contrary, he shared bread with Judas—the same bread that, at that table, Jesus had consecrated as the Eucharist. The patient and, dare we say, optimistic Jesus gave Judas time to repent and change the course of his life.

Nor did Jesus reject Peter after the triple denials; instead, according to Mark's gospel, the angel on Jesus' behalf told the women at the tomb on Easter morning to "go tell the disciples and Peter" that they would see the Lord in Galilee.

Lent is an invitation to us to avoid the willful and pessimistic defection of Judas and imitate instead the resilience of Peter, sharing his confidence that the Lord, even after we have hurt him, is eager to embrace us again as his friends.

ACT

*Take a step toward spiritual growth.*

I will take time to recall what commitments I have made to Christ over the course of my life, ask forgiveness if at any time I have broken my promises, and rededicate myself to the Lord, knowing that he will gladly receive me.

PRAY

Lord Jesus Christ, it pains and saddens us to think of how often you have been betrayed by those to whom you offer inexhaustible love. May we always try earnestly to keep faith with you and live in a way that is worthy of you. Amen.

# WEDNESDAY, APRIL 17
## HOLY WEEK

BEGIN

*Spend a minute or two in silence. Set aside whatever might hinder your prayer.*

PRAY

See, the Lord GOD is my help; who will prove me wrong?

*~Isaiah 50:9a*

LISTEN

*Read Matthew 26:14–25.*

"The Son of Man indeed goes, as it is written of him, but woe to that man by whom the Son of Man is betrayed. It would be better for that man if he had never been born."

*~Matthew 26:24*

## *The Goal Is Heaven*

This day was once known as Spy Wednesday, a reference to the presence of a "spy," Judas, among the apostles. The name flowed from the gospel reading, which focuses on the incident in which Jesus predicts that a disciple will betray him.

But the first reading, the psalm, and the gospel passage taken together look more broadly at the suffering Jesus will undergo. It begins with the betrayal, but the reading from the prophecy of Isaiah anticipates the physical abuse—"I gave my back to those who beat me, my cheeks to those who plucked my beard; My face I did not shield from buffets and spitting" (50:6)—and Psalm 69 looks at the abandonment and humiliation—"I looked for sympathy, but there was none; for consolers, not one could I find. Rather they put gall in my food, and in my thirst they gave me vinegar to drink" (v. 20b–21).

As we prepare to commemorate the Passion of Jesus, the path that led to his Resurrection, we leave Judas to his fate and turn our full attention to Jesus. As we do, we notice the patience with which he endured everything. We, too, are called upon to accept patiently the travails we experience through natural causes or through the thoughtlessness or malice of others.

Patiently accepting problems doesn't mean that we can't complain or grieve—on the contrary, complaining and grieving are important psychological outlets. It does mean, though, that, as Jesus does during his Passion, we should remember that everything we experience in this life, good or bad, is temporary, and that the bad should not discourage us and distract us from the only thing that matters—our own resurrection at the end of this journey and the life we will live forever in the presence of God.

ACT

*Take a step toward spiritual growth.*

When I am troubled by pain or illness, by a personal relationship, or by events taking place in the world, I will try to balance my reaction with my faith in God's promise of eternal life with him.

PRAY

Lord Jesus, may I have faith that my troubles are only temporary obstacles as I fix my gaze on my ultimate goal: life with you in heaven. Amen.

# The Easter Triduum

On these days, it is important to pray together with your parish community. These meditations are brief so that you can spend time participating in the Church's most sacred liturgies.

# Thursday, April 18
## Holy Thursday

LISTEN

*Read John 13:1–15.*

So when he had washed their feet and put his garments back on and reclined at table again, he said to them, "Do you realize what I have done for you? You call me 'teacher' and 'master,' and rightly so, for indeed I am. If I, therefore, the master and teacher, have washed your feet, you ought to wash one another's feet. I have given you a model to follow, so that as I have done for you, you should also do."

*~John 13:12–15*

*I Have Given You a Model*

Former presidents of the United States have taken varied approaches to "retirement." Some have adopted quiet roles as elder statesmen; others have remained very active. John Quincy Adams, for example, spent seventeen years as a member of the House of Representatives, and William Howard Taft served more than eight years as chief justice of the United States.

But the former president who comes to mind in light of today's gospel reading is Jimmy Carter, particularly for his hands-on work with Habitat for Humanity, building houses for the poor in the United States and fourteen other countries, and doing this into his nineties. Carter also engaged in human-rights activism and diplomacy after leaving the White House, but the image of him and his wife, Rosalynn, working in their jeans and Habitat shirts is an apt example of the spirit of Jesus' remarkable act that we commemorate today.

Jesus, although he was their teacher and master, washed the feet of his apostles, and he pointedly told them, and us, that he had set an example that his disciples must follow. Presidents or pedestrians follow him by putting aside any feeling of self-importance in order to serve the needs of friends and strangers.

PRAY

Lord Jesus, you called us to celebrate the Eucharist in memory of you. May we also remember you whenever we learn of a person in need, and may our memorial be an act of compassion and service that imitates your example. Amen.

# FRIDAY, APRIL 19
## GOOD FRIDAY

LISTEN

*Read John 18:1–19:42.*

"For this I was born and for this I came into the world, to testify to the truth. Everyone who belongs to the truth listens to my voice."

*~John 18:37b*

*First to Hear God's Word*

Today, on Passover, we read several times in the gospel passage that "the Jews" called for the death of Jesus.

These references have been used often in history as a justification for persecution of the Jewish people.

As we reflect today on the shameful treatment of Jesus, it is also appropriate to recall what the Second Vatican Council declared in the document *Nostra Aetate*, that the death of Jesus "cannot be charged against all the Jews, without distinction, then alive, nor against the Jews of today." And, especially on Passover, it is suitable to recall the council's teaching, following on the words of St. Paul, that not only are the Jews not to be portrayed as somehow abandoned by God but that God does not repent of the promises he makes and that his covenant with the children of Abraham is an everlasting one.

Catholic Christianity has its roots in the patriarchs and prophets of Judaism and has based its own worship on the scriptures and traditions of the Jewish people. Rather than looking askance at them because of an uncritical reading of the gospels, we should pray for them and pray with them for a better world for everyone.

PRAY

Almighty God, we pray today for the Jewish people, to whom you spoke first, that you may grant them to advance in love of your name and in faithfulness to your covenant. You bestowed your promises on Abraham and his descendants; now hear graciously the prayers of your Church, that the people you first made your own may attain the fullness of redemption. Through Christ our Lord. Amen.

*~Adapted from* The Roman Missal, *third edition*.

# Saturday, April 20
## Holy Saturday

LISTEN

*Read Luke 24:1–12.*

"Why do you seek the living one among the dead?
He is not here, but he has been raised. Remember
what he said to you while he was still in Galilee, that
the Son of Man must be handed over to sinners and
be crucified, and rise on the third day."

*~Luke 24:5b–7*

## *Then Tell the World*

Our experience of this day is different from that of the
first disciples. We anticipate the grinding sound of the
stone rolling away from the tomb, the flash of lightning,
the clap of thunder, the appearance of the risen Lord, his
raiment as white as snow. The first disciples expected
none of that.

For them, this was a day of disappointment, fear,
loneliness—the kind of day the Church evokes by
removing the Eucharist from the tabernacle, stripping
the altar, and veiling the crucifix. Mary Magdalene, the
apostles, and the other disciples felt empty on this day,
and they were shaken to the core by what happened the
following morning. Despite Jesus' predictions, they did
not expect him to rise again.

And it was precisely because of the impact the Resurrection had on them that they were inspired to proclaim to anyone who would listen in any village, city, or
country they could reach in the decades that followed
this day.

Let us spend time this day contemplating the enormity of the astounding truth that out of love for us, God,

in his Son, has overcome both sin and death. And then, let us proclaim it to the world.

# Sunday, April 21
## Easter Sunday

LISTEN

*Read Colossians 3:1–4.*

"If then you were raised with Christ, seek what is above, where Christ is seated at the right hand of God. Think of what is above, not of what is on earth. For you have died, and your life is hidden with Christ in God. When Christ your life appears, then you too will appear with him in glory."